# Small Business

*Blueprint on How to Start and Build a Successful Business from Scratch - Startup, Entrepreneur, and Business Ideas*

has been made to provide accurate, up to date and reliable complete information. No warranties of any kind are expressed or implied. Readers acknowledge that the author is not engaging in the rendering of legal, financial, medical or professional advice.

By reading this document, the reader agrees that under no circumstances are we responsible for any losses, direct or indirect, which are incurred as a result of the use of information contained within this document, including, but not limited to, — errors, omissions, or inaccuracies.

# TABLE OF CONTENTS

# Introduction

Thank you for purchasing the book, 'Small Business: Blueprint on How to start and build a successful Business from Scratch - Startup, Entrepreneur, and Business Ideas'.

It is a great thing that you have decided to start your very own business! But, you need to remember that it is essential that you set it up correctly right from the start; you definitely do not want to start from scratch again! You have to follow a process that will lead you to the best results. A lot of people out there have chosen to set up their own companies on account of being independent in their life. People also enjoy working on something that they are passionate about.

This book covers the process that you will need to follow in order to successfully set up your company. The first step is to register your company! You will definitely have to look at all the regulations that you are required to follow in the country or the state that you are living in at the moment.

This book will take you through every step that you will need to undertake when you are starting your very own start up. You will be guided through testing your business idea, conducting thorough market research and also identifying your business and investment requirements. You have to also make a business plan in order to promote your idea of a start up in front of your potential investors. This book has given you the tips that you could use to ensure that your business plan stands out! You will also be able to learn more about how you can market your idea! All in all, this book acts as the perfect guide for you if you are looking at becoming an entrepreneur.

Thank you for purchasing the book. I hope it helps you.

# Chapter 1

## Is it a Good Time to Start?

This is a question that may be looming in your mind. You may have started to worry about whether or not your idea is the right one and if you will be able to sell it. You should never worry about that! You should definitely work towards creating profits out of your idea! There is never a great time to start. You will need to build your company on your own and see it grow! The year 2011 – 12 proved to be the best year ever since there were close to 450,000 people who had set their own companies and has become successful within no time!

People these days have become adventurous and resourceful! Many students have worked towards turning their knowledge and their talent into identifying a way to make a living. There are others who have broken away from tradition and have decided to set up their own companies in order to be independent. There are quite a few mothers out there who have noticed that there are quite a few gaps in the market and have come up with many ventures! You have to remember that your age can never be a hindrance when you are trying to fulfill your passion. When you decide to begin your business, you will be able to reach out to customers all over the world!

## Three Reasons why you should start a business now

If the reason above has not convinced you to push the question out of your mind, the reasons that have been given in this section of the chapter definitely should!

### Low Start – up costs

There are quite a few businesses all over the world that has begun at an initial or a start – up cost of less than $1000. If you have an app or have a business card in your hand, you will find yourself making sales that surmount your initial costs! You will also be able to set your business operations up at home!

### Growing Technology

There are quite a few social media platforms and other websites that provide various start – ups with the perfect opportunities to set their businesses up directly into the market. You will be able to sell your products and services and also promote them easily and at affordable rates! You can use platforms like Facebook, Instagram, YouTube and Twitter for the same!

## Great levels of support

You will never be alone when you are looking at starting your very own business! You will find yourself with immense support and will grow in no time.

- The public and the private sectors will support you by providing you with the perfect areas where you will be able to set your workstations up.

- The banks and other corporates will be able to help you fund your expenses and invest in your company!

- You have numerous mentors in the market that will be more than happy to impart knowledge about how you will be able to create a successful business in the current market.

Having read the above, are you still skeptical about setting up your very own business? But, there are certain things that you will need to clarify before you set up your company.

## An Entrepreneur – to be or not to be

This section consists of a tiny exercise that you could use to see if you are ready to be an entrepreneur. It may seem like a fun exercise, but if you do work on it seriously, you will be able to know whether or not you are on the right path when it comes to starting your very own business. However, this is only a guide and is not the rule, but this gives you a little bit of an insight about yourself before you plunge into enjoying the independence that comes with self – employment. Every person has an idea on how a typical entrepreneur thinks and behaves. The test consists of questions that are based on the same.

Setting up and running the operations of your business is not something that every person will be able to do. It is a highly stressful job and you may or may not always make a profit! But, there is the positive aspect of you having control of your life! You would never have another person telling you what you must do and how you must do it. But, there is the possibility that you will work longer than you have ever worked in your life! This is because of the fact that you will need to work on making money since you do not have the confidence that your salary will be credited to your account every month. You will find yourself losing your financial security since you will need to cover the overhead expenses for your company before your very own expenses.

If you are looking at benefitting by taking this little test, it would be good if you spent a great deal of time with each question before you choose to answer! You are the only person who is going to look at your answers so it is best if you are brutally honest with yourself. It is an extremely important decision that you are making when it comes to starting your very own business. You have to make sure that your decision is the best decision that you have ever made since this will affect your life! You will find that there are a few questions that mean the same but have been worded slightly differently. Do not mull over the questions, but answer them the way you would answer a regular examination paper. You will know why this is being done for certain! The test is very easy to take. You will have to mark the column on your right with the answer that you believe represents the question. I will tell you how you must score yourself at the end of the quiz. To make it easier, you could print these pages out when you are working at answering the test.

| | Hell Yeah! | Maybe | No | Sorry, what? |
|---|---|---|---|---|
| I am someone who has succeeded at convincing people to believe what I believe in | | | | |
| I am surrounded by people who have supported me in all my ventures | | | | |
| I am someone who finds it easy to communicate with strangers over the phone | | | | |
| I have made many acquaintances who have become great friends over the years | | | | |
| I am a person whom people have always loved | | | | |
| I am terribly impatient and get frustrated when I find people taking their time when it comes to work | | | | |
| I have found myself | | | | |

| | | | | |
|---|---|---|---|---|
| ignoring someone else's opinion if I believed something to be true | | | | |
| I am someone who is often bored | | | | |
| I love identifying new ways to approach a particular problem | | | | |
| I am someone who has always loved the advance in technology | | | | |
| I always look at the bigger picture before worrying about the minute details | | | | |
| I revel in being noticed for the work that I have done | | | | |
| I am a person who has always been trusted by the people around me | | | | |
| I enjoy living simply and have never been depressed by the lack of certain luxuries | | | | |

Once you have answered the questions that have been asked in the above quiz, you should total up the scores. Your score will leave you with the knowledge of whether or not you are fit to be an entrepreneur. If you have received a very low score, you definitely have to wait before you dive into becoming an entrepreneur. If you have found yourself answering yes to all the questions above, you would do well to begin your very own firm. This quiz is just to give you an idea on whether or not you are ready. However, you need to remember that you need to keep motivating yourself! Whatever your score may be, a loss that you may encounter while setting your company up should never let you back down from the plan!

## The Best Business Philosophy

There are a lot of business philosophies that you could use when you are working towards setting up your very own business. It is best if you use the first principles of thinking when you are looking at setting up your company.

The 'first principles of thinking' is a way by which you try to understand the root cause for any problem that you have at hand. You will find that you are able to obtain your solution with ease. You will find yourself becoming successful if you use this philosophy. This is what Elon Musk uses when he plans his businesses and that has always benefited him! He has built rockets for NASA and has also played a great role in building the first ever electric car. He is a visionary who has the wish to colonize Mars.

# Chapter 2

# The Business Ideas in Trend

There are pundits and experienced entrepreneurs who have predicted the different businesses that people should look into when they are considering to set their own business up.

There are quite a few businesses that have the higher chance of faring better than most others in the modern world. If you were looking for ideas and you looked on the Internet, you will find a million ideas. There is a list that is given below which consists of the ideas that have proved to be successful over the last few years! You could use these as a part of your investigation when you are trying to identify the right business for you. This is only if you do not have an idea on what you want to start your business on!

If any of the ideas given below strike you, you could conduct further investigation on them and see if they would benefit you in any way. There are quite a few ideas that you could find within the opportunities that have been mentioned in this chapter. This chapter only covers a little detail about the opportunities.

## Casual Dining

In this fast paced world, people find it very difficult to relax and enjoy a meal. They prefer buying elegant food that is made quickly. They hate having to wait for the food to be prepared and served. However, these foods have to be priced reasonably to ensure that they are not ripped off.

The idea behind casual dining is two – fold; the first is to provide food that is of great quality while the second is service in seconds. The idea of casual dining has been growing at a rapid rate! This is because of the fact that there are different menus that have been created that are charged at different rates. Different classes of the society can afford these rates. You could use food trucks as an idea. There are a lot of food trucks that sell elegant food on their trucks! They charge different foods at different prices.

## Staples for Customers

Every person has to eat well in order to survive. The items that human beings procure and consume often have to be replaced! These are necessary goods that every consumer will have to purchase in order to survive. The demand for these goods never decreases. If you begin to manufacture such items and buy and sell them, you will be able to create the perfect business for yourself!

## Care for the Elder

Here are some facts that you have to know:

1. Over 7 million of the baby boomers turn seventy years of age every single year!

2. A boomer attains the age of seventy every 7 seconds and there are boomers that attain the age of 60 every 10 seconds.

These facts go to say that the people in this century have begun to live longer and healthier lives! They have also learnt to live independently till the age where they find themselves needing the extra help. Since they prefer living in their own homes, they require care. If you set up a company or a business in this industry, you will find that your business growing in the consecutive years.

## Consulting Firms

This is an option that most people choose since this requires the least cost when you plan to set up the company. There are quite a few companies that have fired employees from various departments of from one particular department which they deemed was unnecessary at that point. They have now started outsourcing these requirements to different firms. Many companies have moved from outsourcing these requirements to large corporations and have begun to outsource these requirements to smaller firms or consultancies. The best industries to target would be risk management, finance and investment.

## Fitness and Health

People all over the world have realized that their bodies need to be fit and healthy. They have realized that they need to reduce their weight or work on maintaining a fit body. They love working out at the gym to tone their muscles or lose the excess weight. This industry has gained a lot of importance the last few years and will definitely bring you great fortune in the future!

## Yoga

You may begin to wonder why this has come under a separate industry when it can be included under fitness and health. This was done due to the fact that Americans spent close to $15 billion to purchase yoga equipment, clothing and products. They have claimed that they purchase these items because they have been asked by their therapist or their doctor to begin practicing yoga.

## Improvement of constructions

The changes in the climate have caused a lot of people to move their houses to different locations. They have begun renovating their houses to ensure that their house can sustain the climatic change. People have started making their houses eco – friendly by using solar panels to obtain electricity. This has become the best industry to start a business in since you could either work towards identifying eco – friendly items that could be used to renovate the house, or you could start a construction company providing the material and labor to construct houses.

## Repair Services

Human beings across the world have decided that they would like to repair items and not throw them away when they stop working. This provides you with a wide range of opportunities. You could own a garage or have an electronic goods store. This would prove to be a great boon for any entrepreneur. You could also own a store that provides spare parts for televisions, dishwashers, washing machines and any other electrical appliance!

## Finance and Accounting Services

Most companies have been outsourcing their accounting services since they are unable to handle an entire department to keep their financial books. This business has benefitted many entrepreneurs since they find book keeping an easy job. This is a start – up which has a very low initial cost but has the best potential. There are a lot of businesses that have been started recently. This goes to say that you would never find yourself short of any clients. As the economy builds, there will be more companies entering the market that will ensure that you have clients coming to you more often!

## Apps

There are over 500,000 apps that have been approved by Google and Apple. The Google Play store and the App store for the Apple products have a million apps that have been purchased or downloaded by millions of people. You will be able to make a great deal of money if you are looking at creating an app. For instance, you could create and build an app where a person would be able to know the address of the person whose name they type in on the app. This would fetch you millions. If you need to know more about how you can create an app or how it will benefit you, you could look at a Ted Talk that was given by an app developer who developed an app when he was in the sixth grade – Thomas Suarez.

## E – Commerce websites

You may have wondered why this is an industry that you could try! There are a lot of major domains like Amazon, best Buy and Apple that have grasped the interest of many customers. But, there is a lot of scope in this market! There are a lot of people who peruse through the different options that are available on the Internet when they are looking to buy something. Most people do not have the time to walk into a store and patiently look through things that they can purchase. When they find an online website that provides them with what they need most at the affordable prices, they will jump at the chance and purchase those items. For instance, you could create a website that sells groceries and other household items that are bought most often at the supermarkets. This would be the perfect business idea!

# Chapter 3

# Testing Your Idea

When you have identified what it is that you would like to do, and what products and services you would want to provide for your customers, you will need to test your ideas! This chapter provides you with four steps that you could use in order to test your idea. These steps would help you understand how good your product is and whether or not you have chosen the right market or not!

## Set up a landing page

This is an experiment that you are conducting to test your idea. You should never mistake this page to be the 'We are coming soon' page! There are a few characteristics about a landing page that you will have to know.

Your landing page has to always include the price that you are requesting from your customers in return for your products and services. When you place this on the page you will know if your customers are okay with the price that you are requesting. You will also be able to identify whether your product or service is something that is valuable for them to acknowledge. The price that you place on the website does not have to be the real price of your product or service, but you have to ensure that it is a credible amount. You cannot say $2 on your landing page and then charge them $20. That is ten times the cost and you have cheated your customers. If you would like to try different prices, you could split your landing page and try different numbers to see which brought in the maximum number of customers.

Your landing page must also give your customers the belief that the product already exists! You should use links that would help them purchase the product. The landing page should bring them to the main website to purchase the product. If you have a product or service that you are selling for free, you could see whether your customers are willing to go the extra mile and provide you with extra information or whether they are willing to download the app to remain in touch with you. You will have to provide a description of your product and also explain to them how it will help them. You will have to complete your landing page while giving your customers an impression that they can definitely trust you!

## Define what Success is to you

Let us assume that your landing page has helped you receive 100 sign ups in two days. Do you believe that this is good news? Or do you think you have failed? You will never know this unless you have set a certain standard for yourself. What is the least number of sign ups you need in order to give you the confidence to carry your idea forward?

You have to ensure that you base the success you achieve based on certain factors. You will have to identify the opportunity cost of you starting your business, the cost of development and also the KPIs of business. You have to identify the number of sign ups that you will need in order to be able to generate the revenue that you are looking for. You have to make sure that you have defined what success means to you before you have begun your experiment. You should ensure that you are not someone who is running after results that you have not been able to achieve.

## Show yourself to your customers

When your page is ready, you will have to find the right customers and appear in front of them. The best way to do this is through Google Adwords. You will be able to identify and target the right traffic and be able to test your product and service. You will find certain tools using which you will be able to create and launch a Google advertisement in less than two minutes. If you want to use this technology well, you will have to choose the best phrases and keywords that will match your product and service. It is best to not use generic terms.

## Follow Up

When you have conducted your experiment, try and analyze the data that you have collected at the end of the experiment. Did you not receive the number of sign ups that you had expected? Or did you receive more than what you had expected? You will need to follow up with the people who did sign up and try to understand what they expect about your company and what they expect from the product and service. You will have to understand their enthusiasm and also identify if the idea that you have decided to follow through with will meet their expectations. You will have to see how much you are spending on trying to acquire customers and how much you may make in the future. You could adjust your pricing based on the same. If you find that you have made no profit at all, you will thank the experiment since you have just saved yourself from losing billions of dollars working towards building something that would have not brought you any sort of revenue. You can now test another idea.

# Chapter 4

## Understanding Your Market and the Requirements of Business – Market Analysis and Report

With all the work that you have to do to test your idea, you will have to also understand the type of business and market you are getting into. You will have to work towards trying to understand what kind of a workplace you are looking for and also the labor that you will need to procure for the same.

This is something that plays a key role in your business plan. This is the section that your investors will look into when you approach them for finances. You will have to also talk about how your product and service is unique when compared to other companies in the same market.

It does not matter what type of market you have chosen to enter, but you have to ensure that you conduct thorough market research to understand the business better. You would also be able to estimate the requirements of your business through this process. You will have to focus on the following aspects while conducting market research.

1. Market Participants

2. The patterns of distribution

3. Competitors

This chapter provides you with detailed information on what you will need to consider while working on the different aspects of market research.

## Market Analysis

So what is market research? Market research or analysis is a method by which you observe the market closely to understand its dynamics and its characteristics. The problem is the most people assume that one must begin doing market research only after one has completed one's production and is thinking about distribution. This is the worst approach to business possible.

As a start up entrepreneur, you need to conduct market research at every stage of your business. Even when you are just thinking about starting a business, you must conduct market analysis to make sure that your idea will be feasible – as we saw in the previous chapter, to be able to come up with an idea itself, you need to know what the current market trends are. Based on the facts and figures that you collect, you can then go about setting up a business that falls in line with the existing trends in the market.

Just as you must conduct market research at the beginning of your business idea, you also need to continue doing analysis of market trends throughout your business process. As you are building your business profile and your business plan to actually get into the nitty and gritty details of how to produce, how to distribute and then make sales, keep doing your research to understand the market dynamics.

For instance, you will need to ask yourself questions like who is the biggest supplier of my product in the current market? Obviously, this person is your competitor, so how will your product outshine his? In what way is yours better? What is the distribution pattern of your goods? How can you make it more cost effective while still meeting all the market requirements?

Can you see how you need to answer these questions before you even get into the production of your product? Obviously, you need to constantly keep yourself up to date with the market trends and changes – beware! The only constant about the market is that it is a constantly shifting entity; what is in fashion today will be outdated tomorrow and you and your company must stay on your toes to meet the consumers' requirements.

I must place a lot of emphasis laid on how well you can use the Internet to obtain information. The advantage with the Internet is that you do not have to make an extra effort to learning more about a particular business. A vast majority of the population knows how they can use the Internet to obtain all the information that they need. After the explosion of information in the year 1990, people have found it terribly easy to gather any kind of information. There exists a problem to know how you can sort the information.

There are a lot of websites that have information on just about anything! You will find yourself with lots of help when you are looking at identifying the perfect market that you should enter. You will also be able to learn more about marketing strategies and will also be able to stay in touch with your customers through the Internet.

All of this sounds extremely vague and very out there, I know. So how do you quantify your terms and where do you start exactly? I'll tell you – you need to begin by assessing your own company first. Or what you think your company will be like, in this case, given that you only have a skeletal framework of it. For this assessment, you need to start by doing a SWOT analysis.

SWOT – Strengths, Weaknesses, Opportunities and Threats – Analysis is the basis of any company's business plan. Step back and take an objective look at what your strengths are. What is it that you have to offer the market and the general public? How does your product or service do in comparison to the giants in the industry and what is the something special you have to offer to your customers and other stakeholders?

Look at your weaknesses with an equally sharp eye. Where are your weak spots? Is it in the marketing? Is it in the financing? Do you have enough labor force to carry you through? Do you lack investment or are you weak in advertising? Figure out where you will need extra help and focus on strengthening those areas.

Opportunities and Threats, on the other hand, are more of an external analysis than an internal one. Look at the environment and the market that surrounds you. What are the opportunities you can make use of for your company? What are the threats you are likely to face? Again, it sounds vague; so let me give you an example to quantify these terms better. Let us say that there is a local carnival happening in town and you are a regular sponsor for it. Like every year, this year too you have been asked to donate some money to set it up. This is an excellent opportunity to gain visibility for your business! Find out if you – as a sponsor – will be allowed to put up a stall of your own or if you, your company name and your company logo can be featured on the carnival banner. It is an opportunity to convince people about your business, so do not let that go!

A threat, contrarily, could cripple your business. Say, for instance, that your community is standing on the cusp of a new leadership – the elections are currently taking place as your business has just begun. You will need to carefully analyze the business and economic policies of all the prospective leaders to ensure that your company will not suffer. If, for instance, your business is based on import and export of goods, the candidates' foreign policies could pose a potential threat to you, especially if they come into power after you have become established. You may need to change all your procedures all over again. It might be a good idea to wait until elections are over, see who the new candidate is and then go about setting up your new business venture.

Do you see the difference between strengths, weaknesses, opportunities and threats now? This is where you begin – by assessing both the internal and the external circumstances and abilities of your company, you are quantifying your business plan and solidifying your idea into a strong reality that you can establish and build a legacy on. Once you complete your SWOT Analysis, you will know the position of your company in relation to its external and internal environments and you can focus on building a business plan that is customized to suit your needs. If, for instance, you have ample investment and employees that are wonderful at advertising, then you need to focus on making those the primary strengths of your business strategy! In fact, in this situation, you can even think of setting up an ad agency or a marketing consultancy firm instead of producing and distributing – that is how you turn your strengths into opportunities of your own.

After you complete your SWOT Analysis, you will need to extend it into a full and proper market analysis. Start by doing a preliminary research that will consist of the following.

## Market Participants

This is an important component that helps to describe what type of business you are by talking about the nature of the different participants in the market. This is an important fact to know since there are a lot of participants who have products and services that have different variations. For instance, there are certain companies that are monopolies, implying that there are no other participants in the industry anywhere else in the world.

This information would definitely make a difference to your business and the plan that you have for your business. There are certain industries, like the dry cleaning industry, that have million participants all across the world. You could say the same about the food industry as well. However, there is a certain area in the food industry, the fast food industry, which has a lot of scope although there are a lot of other competitors.

Economists have coined a term called consolidation that is defined as the phase after which certain companies grow and become multinational companies and surpass the smaller companies. These small companies would eventually disappear from the market. You could see this happen in any industry! Consider a supermarket in your neighborhood. If a mall were to be constructed near the supermarket, you will find that every person in your neighborhood has stopped going to the supermarket and has started spending more time at the mall.

## Identify the patterns of distribution

Once you have identified the way the market works, you will have to start identifying how the other companies in the market distribute their products and services. You have to try to identify whether you will need to outsource the distribution to retailers or other stores. For instance, if you own a company that manufactures woolen clothes, you will need to identify a retailer who would be willing to sell your product. This is the same for most markets. If you can support your own sales, you will be able to avoid finding a retailer. But, if you do not think you can support your sales, you will have to find representatives who will be able to help you in selling your services and products.

There are quite a few products that have always been sold in retail stores. There are certain products that have always been purchased by the manufacturers from the distributors and sold to the right consumers. There are times when the manufacturer has direct contact with the consumer and sells the product that you manufacture. The manufacturer could help you by starting a campaign on the Internet that provides wide access to consumers who are interested in the products and services that you sell.

You will find that there are different products that are distributed in different ways. You can choose to distribute your products through door – to – door sales or you could advertise your products and services through different media. You could then sell the products directly after manufacturing them.

There are other products that you will be able to sell directly through the business. The perfect example for the same would be the relationship that the suppliers of the parts for cars and the manufacturers of those cars share. There are some companies that employ agents or representatives to distribute and sell their products. There are recent advances in technology that help in the wider distribution of certain products and services.

## Identify the competition

You will need to work on conducting the perfect research to identify the competition that you have in the market. This is where you will be able to understand what the market is all about and also will be able to understand the business that you have chosen better. You will also be able to know what the strengths and weaknesses are of the industry.

What do you think are the key characteristics of success? What do you think are the unique characteristics of products and services that make them easier to sell over others? The competition always depends on the trend and the reputation of the company in the market. The distribution channels are what make the most difference when it comes to understanding the level of competition.

When you look at the food industry, you will find that the competition is dependent on the idea or view that the consumers have about the market. For instance, consider a chef who has studied in Cordon Bleu while there is another home cook. Whom would a restaurant hire? They would hire the chef from Cordon Bleu since that is a reputed institute.

In most professional services, you would have to be wary about the marketing that happens through word of mouth. Why would people approach a caterer to provide food for a certain event and not cook themselves? Why would they want to approach a wedding planner instead of planning their own wedding? Why do people hire certain architects to design their house instead of doing it on their own?

**Identify your main competitors!**

This is a step that gives you the best idea about the market! When you are looking at a certain market, there will be someone who is already prominent in the market. You will need to identify those companies and ensure that you know the company well. For instance, if you have decided to start an e – commerce website, you will have to look at other websites and see what is different about yours. You will also be able to identify the strengths and weaknesses of your competitors and your company too. You will also have to see what type of technology they have been using when it comes to selling their products. You have to also check how or why they pose a threat to your company!

## Understanding the Business Requirements

You will have to look at what your business needs most! This section covers what you need to identify.

1. You will have to see how what raw material and equipment you will need to produce your product or service

2. You will have to identify the type of labor that you will have to employ. You will know the qualification that you need to know

3. You will also have to identify the location where you would want to establish your business. This is an essential aspect to remember.

When you are trying to assess this, you will also have to assess the cost of the items that you will need in order to approach your investors with the financial plan. You should use the 'first principles of thinking' when it comes to identifying the cost of your raw material. For instance, let us assume that you looking at manufacturing woolen products. You would need labor or you would need machines for the manufacturing of the woolen products.

If you were to use labor for the same, you would have to identify the number of people you would need to hire and also the amount you would have to pay them in order to keep them working for you. Break down all your costs to the nitty gritty details to identify the actual cost that you would incur. This is what Elon Musk had done when he had decided to start building rockets. He broke down the cost of the rockets to the nitty gritty details to identify the actual cost that he would have to incur when he had decided to first start his company, SpaceX.

All these aspects are just the beginning of your proper research into the market. What we have done so far is an extremely skeletal market analysis that is just the beginning. The dimensions of an actual, proper market research report are many in number; so far, you have simply taken a look at the most immediate factors that will affect your business. Now you need to go into further detail, take a closer look and examine all the factors so that you customize them to suit your particular business needs.

## Dimensions of a Full Market Analysis

As I said, to be able to become a successful entrepreneur, you need to complete a full market analysis before you even begin setting up your company. Here are the factors you will need to look into.

*Size of the Market* - How big are you aiming your market to be? Obviously, when we were looking at the market participants earlier, you would have realized that the bigger your market, the more number of competitors you have. And let us face it – as a small entrepreneur who is just setting up a business venture, you will not be ready to face off against the giants in the industry right away, even if you are brilliant and have the finances to do so! You need to establish yourself first and build brand loyalty and you must start by doing this locally.

Restrict the size and scale of your market to a realistic margin. For instance, if you are setting up a local organic foods store, scale your market size down to the whole of your community and locality. Now, step back and analyze the market trends, competitors, distribution and the like. What do your customers like? Where do they generally buy from? Who is your major competitor and what advantage or disadvantage does he have over you? How can you compete with this?

Do you see how customized each market then becomes? To increase your consumer base and build brand loyalty, you will need to get extremely specific with your research and analysis. Different markets will have different trends; what sells in the United States of America will definitely not sell as easily in Africa or even Asia. When you scale it further down, what sells in New York will not be as easy to market in Texas. To make sure your pricing policy, your marketing strategy, your overall business plan falls into place, figure out your market size. It may seem small initially, but capture that small market share first – you can slowly increase your market size as you get past your break-even point and then grow and expand further.

*Growth Rate of your Market* - Whether your market will grow and just how fast it will grow is something you need to take into account when you conduct your market analysis. This is to help you identify how long your prospective market share will remain yours; obviously, before you decide to spend a whole lot of cash and invest in something, you need to analyze and see if and how much it will grow over the projected period of time you are planning on investing for.

The rate at which your market grows usually depends on the current trends at present. You want to make sure that the products you are offering will remain in fashion ten years from now; you do not want you or your company becoming obsolete and then bankrupt. If the business idea does not have a market growth rate with any kind of potential, you may want to switch over to something else to ensure that you will not end up losing all your money.

So how do you define the market growth as such? It is simple, really – you can define it as the increase in sales that is seen within a selected group of consumers within a limited and specified time frame. Obviously, as a start up company, you will not have not have sales of your own as of yet. In this case, what you need to do is to conduct an analysis of the growth rate of already existing companies to study the market trends. That will let you know what the potential growth rate for you is and where possibilities exist for you to capture a market share of your own.

Think about how much percentage of your target market you want to begin with and then make them grow. Let us say, for instance, that you are opening an upscale, high-end restaurant in your locality. Is the number of people who go to these people plenty in number in your area? Are they increasing or decreasing and by what numbers? How much of your competition lies within that greasy fast food and burger joint directly across the street? How many customers a day do you lose to them and how can you tackle this problem?

Start your report by making a market growth rate forecast; find out the total numbers as it stands today with the number of possible and prospective customers in each segment before you identify the projected percentage within the next three to five years based on the average growth rate of other companies in the vicinity in the past few years. Also mention your particular competitive advantage over these companies so that you will be able to convince prospective financial backers.

*Trends Present in the Market* - I have already mentioned this a number of times in the previous sections, but that I keep reiterating the idea should tell you how important and relevant it is. Any kind of market analysis is based on the trends present in the market at a given time. As we already discussed, if you do not know what is popular within the market at the current time, you will not be able to sell your product or even design a product to distribute.

Conducting an investigation into what the consumers like and what the current market demands are is a brilliant way to begin a start up – it will let you see what the requirement is in the economy. And when you know what the need is, you can easily go about fulfilling it by setting up a company to do so. Sales will become easier and you can build brand loyalty much faster when you cater to the needs of an entire community based on whose personal opinion your entire company has been built.

You will have to answer questions like these to find out the current market trends – what do your customers like the most? How much are they willing to spend and how far are they willing to go get what they like? From your observation of their needs and demands from the past few years, what do you predict is going to be their likes and wants within the next few years?

You will also need to study your competitors' moves and see how they have responded to changing market trends. Take for instance the marketing strategy. Over the years, the introduction of technology and social media has completely and utterly changed the face of marketing and advertising strategies. So if you run an ad agency – the current market trend is to advertise and engage with customers on social platforms such as Instagram, Facebook, Twitter and the like. So your market trend analysis must include these; how many of your competitors and customers have access to these platforms? What is the reach of these platforms? How much of the market share has your competitor captured by making use of these platforms? Your personal business plan will change based on the answer to all these questions.

Keep in mind that the only thing constant about the market and its trends is that it keeps changing. What was in fashion yesterday is obsolete today. For instance, producers of flip phones or landline phones who have not upgraded to selling smart phones have been left in the dust simply because the number of people who use these have become extremely small in number. The market is a treacherous place, constantly changing, which is why market and trend analysis must be done regularly. Even after you have begun selling your product, even after you have become established and built brand loyalty, you have to keep conducting a trend analysis to ensure that your customers stay and become repeat customers instead of the single buy off.

Also remember that changing market trends provide and excellent opportunity to expand your business. If, for example, you are running a pet store and the current rage in your vicinity is rescuing homeless animals, maybe you could consider adding a homeless wing shelter to your store. You can also add value added services like veterinary services at a discounted price for those who get involved with rescue efforts – this will not only get you visibility and advertising, it will also fulfill your corporate social responsibility and endear you to your people.

If you are the kind of person who prefers to stick to producing and selling a singular type of product, changing market trends could pose as a serious threat to you. You will need to be extra careful and on your toes; you cannot be rigid or unmoving as an entrepreneur or your company will sink. If you think you cannot keep up with the constant flux and shift in the market, maybe you should step back and reconsider your options before you delve into business.

*Profitability of the Market* - This is one of the most important things to take into account when doing market analysis. As you know, when you start a business enterprise, your prime motive is to make a profit. That is not to say that you are exempt from social responsibility, only that you need to earn a living and expand your business, so profit is definitely your number priority within the limits of legality and what is right.

That means how profitable your venture is going to be is something you will have to analyze extremely carefully. You do not want to put in a huge amount of capital and then end up with a loss because you did not assess the profitability of your company; also keep in mind that, in all likelihood, it is not just your money that would go to waste. We will look at financing options at a later chapter, but suffice to say, as a start up entrepreneur, you will probably have to borrow some money from external sources and you do not want to become indebted to your investors because your profitability quotient was low. Some investors will insist on a projected earnings report including the growth rate and profitability in any case, so you cannot escape this part of market analysis.

So how do you conduct a profitability analysis? First, how do you define market profitability? It sounds easy enough to understand, but it is actually a rather complex and technical term that is too often used in a broad and generic sense. Market profitability is actually understood as all gamut of those financial factors that play an incidental role in the company's ability to make money, once you deduct all the overhead expenses such as the salaries you pay to your employees and the rent you pay on your office utilities. This means that, as a start up company, you will need to assess your current market and then come up with a projected profitability quotient.

To conduct a profitability analysis, you can follow the most basic model of market profitability called *'Porter's Five Forces'*. This was developed by a man named Michael Porter and takes into account the following five factors –

1.  **Buyer Power** – As you can probably guess, this refers to how much influence your customers exert over your chosen market. Each local market and the relationship it shares with its buyers will be very different; circumstances and situations are not the same over the world, after all. When, in a locality, there are many sellers of the same product and there are very few buyers, then the power the buyers hold over that market is enormous. As one of many, you need to set yourself apart from the crowd to appeal to the few customers that both you and your competitors share. Obviously, this means that the prices and the value added services the buyers want, you may have to give.

On the other hand, if you are one of the few sellers within the area selling a product that a large number of buyers require, then obviously, you are more in control. You can afford to determine your own prices and then exert more influence over the buyers rather than the other way around. Thus, how much influence the buyer exerts over the market makes a difference to your business strategy, particularly your pricing policies, thereby affecting your overall profitability.

Conduct a survey within your prospective market area to see where you stand in terms of buyer influence. How popular is the product you want to sell? How many sellers in the area and how many buyers? How essential is it to the peoples' lifestyles? If it is a luxury product instead of a daily consumer good, then what can you do to convince your buyer that they should buy it rather than ignore it for 'at a later time'? Answer all these questions and see how much your buyers are going to affect your projected profitability rates in the future.

2. **Supplier Power** – As you can probably tell, this is similar to buyer power, only here, *you* are the buyer and what you need to identify is how much influence your supplier holds over your particular market share. Obviously, this control is indirect in that they control the movement of your goods and services.

Suppliers are those people who provide you with your raw materials and other goods you need to begin your production process. For instance, if you outsource your labor force itself, then the person whose firm you make use of to get more workers becomes a supplier. It is not just the raw material for your product that you need to find suppliers for; sometimes, even the person who gives you the machinery you need to put these raw materials together is a supplier.

As you can guess, you have to make use of the best supplier who will give you good quality items at optimum cost. This is the ideal case scenario that in reality always does not work out. Your profitability margin will be affected by the cost price these suppliers charge; the more the number of suppliers of your raw material in the market, the more opportunity for price negotiation you have. It is the same principle as the buyer power; this time round, *you* are the buyer, which means that you exert an influence over his business.

However, do keep in mind that the corollary is also true – if the number of suppliers in the market are low and/or if changing suppliers is going to prove a costly effort, then chances are that your suppliers will increase their prices. As is obvious, that will make a difference to your overall profitability margin.

So what you should do is sit down and make a note of all potential suppliers in the vicinity. Do a comparative cost analysis of all the available suppliers and see which one will give you the competitive cost advantage that will help you increase your profitability margin before you approach them. As much as possible, try to negotiate for a lower rate; more often than not, the suppliers want you to bargain and will purposefully quote a high initial price that you must haggle down to an optimum level that is profitable for the both of you.

3. **Barriers to Entry** – Do you remember how we were looking at threats in the SWOT Analysis you started out with? Barriers to entry are something similar; only here, we are looking at the factors that pose a threat into your entry into the already established market. Remember, no matter what product you introduce to the market, some older or similar product already exists – you need to offer something new, something additional to capture market share. This means that there will be definite barriers, which can range anywhere between a hostile economic policy by the government to a low capital investment on your part.

Obviously, the lesser the number of barriers to your entry, the easier it is for you to set up your business and establish your name and logo. The more the number of barriers, the more difficult it is to build a successful company. Let me give you a few examples of the most common barriers to entry.

Capital investment can be a huge problem; in fact, most beginner entrepreneurs cite this as the reason for not opening up their business. This is especially true of a manufacturing company; you will need a lot of cash to buy equipment, raw material, set up your factory and then go through the production process itself. This can be a barrier to your entry into the market, simply because you do not have enough money.

Customer loyalty is also another huge barrier to entry into the market, particularly in monopoly markets. If an already established firm has captured a huge amount of your local market share, that can pose a serious threat to your start up simply because the consumers will prefer to buy from a brand they trust than go to a start up business that has comparatively lesser experience. This means that you will have to work harder, longer and offer them something extra to invite them to you instead of the bigger and more experienced firm. That usually means more investment in terms of time, effort as well as money, so that is something that will have a definite effect on your profitability margin. You must plan for the extra costs and take that into account when you calculate projected profitability.

Intellectual property can be another barrier to entry; if, for instance, the product you want to manufacture and sell has been trademarked or patented by a particular monopoly power, you may have to think about something else instead. Usually, though, patents are given to firms for a limited time period so that they may establish themselves in the market during that time, so you will either have to wait that time out, come up with a newer twist to it so that it does not encroach upon the patent or move on to something else entirely so that you can actually enter into the market with a real product and build your business.

As you can see, there are many different barriers to entering the market – they can be anything! And obviously, you cannot predict each and every one. But there is a rough net that you can cast and within the scope of this net, try to identify the potential barriers that pose a threat to your entry into the market. Check to see how much it will cost you to go beyond this barrier and take that extra price into account while calculating your projected market profitability.

4. **Threat of Substitute Goods and Services** – As the name itself suggests, this category covers that entire list of goods services that can be used in place of the products you are offering to your customers for a number of reasons. These substitute products pose a serious threat not just to you but to your competitors as well; in a way, they are a threat to the whole industry and cannot be ignore when you calculate profitability.

Let me give you an example. If, for instance, you are thinking about going into the production and sale of soda, then you will have to look at the diet fads and trend in the industry. With the growing emphasis on healthier living and replacing junk food with healthier options, chances are that your customers could switch over from soda to plain water or even fruit juice. So these products could pose threat to your business since they could replace you and act as a substitute for you.

Or, here is another example. With the growing rage of social media and Internet video watching, the television is fast becoming obsolete. For instance, a lot of people prefer to watch TV Shows on Netflix rather than when the episodes air on TV itself, leading to the launch of shows that have been released entirely on Netflix instead of ever coming to the TV at all. If this trend continues, then in a few years, chances are that the TV will become obsolete and be replaced by Internet video – people can watch their favorite shows wherever they want, whenever they want and how many ever times they want, all at a nominal subscription rate. Do you see how the substitute product poses a serious threat to the existing product?

Remember, the easier it is for a prospective customer to switch to the alternative good or service, the bigger the threat to your business the item poses. Your marketing strategy will have to take it into account – this means that your profitability ratio cannot ignore these products and must identify how to deal with them. How much extra cost will you incur and how does that factor into your overall market profitability?

5. **Rivalry within Competitors** – As you probably guess, this is simply the market share of your rivals in comparison to yours and how much that is going to affect your overall market profitability. There are a number of factors that affect this idea; for instance, if a product is similar to your but not exactly the same, then that product is definitely your rival. Then, what is the cost of competing with that company? How does it fit into your budget and how much will affect your overall figures?

Ideally, the less competitive the market, the better for you. In any competitive industry, your profits will be low – especially at the beginning – since the customers have the option of approaching your rival if they are not convinced about the price you put up your product at.

Remember, this factor is focused only on the price of the products; when we say rivalry between competitors in terms of profitability quotient, we are talking of the compctitive pricing options that different companies will offer and how that will affect your own pricing policy and overall profitability margin. If, for instance, the competitors around you are not focused on competing on price, then it is possible that you do not have rivalry, but you will have competition in other factors, such as quality and packaging.

So the pricing policy of your rivals makes a huge difference to your own profitability; analyze the trends of the rival company's pricing methodology and try to predict their movements. Take into account their profitability so that you can calculate your own without hassle.

These are the five major factors you must take into account when you calculate the profitability of your company. As I said, you – as a start up business – are more likely to do projected earnings and profitability report, so leave room in your analysis for flexibility so that you can adapt to changes in market trends over the next couple of years. The profitability analysis will help you understand your business's financial health – when you identify the factors that influence your target market and how they affect your own business, you can make sure that you have that competitive edge over your rivals and remain successful.

*Key Factors for Success* - When you do a profitability profile for your company, you need to take into account all factors. These are those aspects that do not really fall into any of the other categories, but nonetheless need to be observed and looked at closely. These are the factors that help you stand out from the rest of your competitors – they can range from anything between the quality of your raw material to the packaging that is unique to you and your brand.

Generally, there are three main ideas that are accepted as key factors to a company's success. These are as follows –

- **Progress of Technology** – As you know, technology is a field that is constantly in a state of flux; it keeps changing and upgrading itself by the day. Where once mobile phones were a luxury for the rich alone, today they are a necessity for every single person. It goes without saying that you need to be on top of the changes in technology as it progresses – you need to not only keep up to date with it, but also start looking for ways to use it for business. For instance, you need to adapt your marketing strategy to make social media marketing on places like Facebook, Twitter and Instagram commonplace for your venture. If there is a newer technology that makes your production process easier or faster or cheaper, you need to switch over to it so that you can gain that competitive edge over your rivals. So in terms of working out your company's profitability, you will have to predict possible changes in technology and how this might affect your business and how you can plan for it.

- **Economies of Scale** – This is a very simple economic term that you should be familiar with. An economy of scale is a business venture in which the cost of producing a single unit of your product becomes cheaper as you expand. Of course, there is more to it than that – you can further look it up online – but it basically boils down to the fact that you attain a cost advantage over your competitors and your overall operational efficiency increases. This kind of an economy of scale is what you need to aim to build – it gives you a clear cost advantage and competitive edge over your rivals and helps you become more firmly established in the market. In terms of profitability profile, for a start up, you need to identify when you will reach the point where your costs per unit of output will become lower in comparison and when you can officially become and economy of scale.

- **Optimum Utilization of Resources** – This is obviously one of the easiest and most important aspects of profitability. You need to make both effective and efficient use of the resources that are at your disposal. It goes without saying that these resources are limited in number; you need to carefully take into account the pros and cons of using them and put each resource to the best possible use so that your business will flourish. In your profitability profile, you must examine the various ways in which you can use the resources and using what resource in which manner will benefit you the most financially.

There are a number of other key success factors, but start by examining these three for now. As you grow and expand further, you yourself will be able to identify other aspects on your own.

*Channels of Distribution* - We have already discussed this in great detail in the previous section. You identified the possible channels of distribution for your product and why should use that particular channel. Another thing you need to think about is what distribution channel your competitor and rivals are making use of; compare it to your own and see if which one of you has the competitive advantage. It will help you identify where you are going wrong and fix things if you need to.

You can also try to develop whole new channels of distribution on your own; the traditional routes are the producer to wholesale markets to retail markets to the consumers. You can eliminate your costs and the middlemen and reach your customers directly by trying out online marketing or selling your own products via your company websites. Try out different strategies and see which one will suit your product and company the best.

*Industry Cost Structure* - Again, this is a bit technical, so bear with me here. In essence, this aspect of market analysis is about how much it will cost overall to get your product from its production stage to sale. The idea is that different industries will have a different cost structure based on the nature of the product they are selling.

In general, there are two accepted types of industries – capital or material intensive industries and labor-intensive industries. The former type is usually where there is heavy manufacturing involved and the production process requires quite a bit of heavy lifting with equipment and capital asset investment. On the other hand, the labor intensive industry is more geared towards service oriented product delivery – consultancy firms, ad agencies and the like, that are based on peoples' skills rather than machine work tend to fall under this category. Of course, this is not a hard and fast line; it is simply a rule of thumb to make identification easier.

Now, when doing a market analysis, you need to take into account the overall cost of your entire process. What are your biggest expenses? What is the overall cost structure in your industry? In a manufacturing unit, which is definitely capital intensive, a majority of the costs would go into raw material acquisition and production. In this case, your overall business strategy should focus on being able to manage your resources effectively so that this initial investment does not go to waste.

In an ad agency, on the other hand, the raw material is the employees' minds. The overhead expenses such as electricity, office stationary and the like will your major expenses and these are what you will have to focus on. Your business strategy then, will be geared towards enabling your employees to think better and perform better, in which case you will have to think about mental stimulation activities such as mind games and the like.

You must also analyze the market trends and identify your competitors' cost structure. Obviously, their books are not open to the public, but whatever information that is available to the public eye, try to compare your standing with theirs to see who has the competitive edge. That way you know where you will need to improve. Ultimately, you must aim at reducing costs without tarnishing quality or creating dissonance amongst your employees – it circles back to the idea of using your resources in the best possible manner to get that extra edge over every other person within the market.

## Building a Consumer Profile

As you can guess, this is one of the most important parts of conducting a Market Analysis, which is why I have put it under a subheading all on its own. Over the years, the motto of business has shifted from power on the sellers' sides to the motto of *'Customer is King'*. This, in essence, boils down to the fact that your consumer is the most important stakeholder for your start up firm and you must do all that you can to keep them satisfied and returning to you. After all, you exist because you want to sell a product to them.

The problem with most entrepreneurs, especially the start up businessmen, is that they hold this belief that the entire locality is your market and every person is a potential customer. This is a big myth! Each business and each product has a target market – you cannot sell a pair of running shoes that cost $10,000 dollars to a man who cannot walk or a man whose monthly income is $1000. People have various factors that influence their buying choices as well as their buying power – you must examine these factors to see who can and will buy your products and aim towards increasing sales amongst this mass crowd.

In essence, you must build the profile of an ideal customer. Now, for an existing business, this is relatively easy; as a start up, you can only pen down what you envision to be your ideal consumer and provide your stakeholders with a projected marketing strategy to capture this segment's interest. So here is how you go about building a consumer profile –

**Step #1** – Understand your own product and its use in the market. We have already touched upon this a little bit in the earlier sections, but to reiterate, look at what you are producing and selling and see what kind of treatment it receives from your customers. How are they intended to be used? How are they actually being used in reality?

What product you offer decides what types of people make use of them; or it can also be the other way around. As we said, you could do an analysis of the market and then decide to cater to a specific section that wants a specific need; in any case, you will have a very specific set of people you must focus on and these people are your target audience. So pay close attention to how your products and services are likely to be used; analyze the sales pattern of the companies that already exist whose records are for public perusal and identify the changing patterns and trends in the product's usage.

**Step #2** – Describe your customers. Now that you have seen how your product is likely to be received in the market, who are the people likely to buy them? Remember, there are different factors that govern a person's ability and choice to buy a product or a service. These may range between likes and dislikes to requirements and budgets. Categorize these general factors and then describe the characteristics of the people that fall into these categories. Here is a simple set of classifications you can do to make the process easier –

- *Demographics* – In this, classify customers according to their demographic profiles such as their ideal age, their gender, their income, etc. For instance, you will find it easier to sell a videogame to a teenager than to a grandparent. Or a consumer whose budget is tight due to a low income will definitely choose to go for a cheaper product. Thus, you must identify the demographic characteristics of your target market so that your marketing strategy can get that much more specific.

- *Psychographics* – This is a bit more complicated in that you must delve into the minds of your customers. This where you list out your ideal customer's personality type, their value systems, their attitudes and interests, etc. Obviously, you cannot predict every person; that is impossible! And you cannot get as specific as you like with this since this all mostly conjecture. This is why studying the patterns of consumers in the industry itself will help; the facts and figures will help you come up with realistic projections so long as you leave room for that small margin of error. Take a look at the statistics of people who have been buying products similar to the ones you want to sell; how is their consumer behavior? What patterns do you observe in their buying and selling choices? What does it say about their psychographic profiles? Take all these details down and then build your own profile.

- *Behavioral Quantification* – This is very similar to the previous idea and can even be considered an extension of it. In this, you must examine the daily behaviors of your ideal customers and identify their lifestyle choices. What behaviors are consistent in their daily lifestyle? If, for instance, you run a transport company, you must ask questions like – do they take public transport or do they drive their own vehicles to work each day? See what their regular habits are and how you can use those to your advantage.

- *Environment and Societal Quantification* – This is, perhaps, a flimsier quantification than the rest, but it is no less important! The environment we live in definitely affects our purchasing power and choices; sometimes, customers may want to buy something that is out of their price range because it will bring them a higher social standing among their peers! This is a set of people that you cannot ignore – you must ask questions like how much can they afford to buy and how hard can you push them to buy – to take them into account when building your ideal customer's profile.

**Step #3** – Locate your customers. This has two aspects to it. One is of course, figuring out where your customers are physically located so that you can sell your product and focus your distribution lines based on their geographical location. If, for instance, you run an online store and your customer lives in another country, shipping options are something you will need to look at closely, along with customs duties and the like. You must also identify who the local sellers of your product in the customers' area are and how you will compete against those companies. This can be especially difficult if your customers are located in a geographically different area that you have very little control over.

The second aspect is to identify where your customers gather in a large group so that advertising and marketing opportunities can be fully utilized. Answer the following questions –

- *Do* your target customers hang out together in large groups regularly?

- If yes, where is this local hang out?

- Will you be able to advertise at this place regularly?

- If yes, what type of advertisements will you be able to put up here?

Identify all these details in connection to where your customer is located and then build their profile further.

**Step #4** – Understand their purchasing process and power. As we said earlier, your customers may or may not buy your product based on a number of factors. Quantify these factors under this heading; try to understand why they buy the product they do and how you factor into this purchasing decision. Ask yourself the following questions –

- What need are they fulfilling with their purchase?

- Do they do research before they choose to buy a product or is it a random and impulsive decision?

- If they do conduct research, how do they go about it? Where do they begin?

- What do they look for within the purchase? Are they focused on price, quality, delivery, packaging, etc? Which factor attracts them the most and why?

Conduct a survey among your local potential consumers and then see what they have to say about these things.

**Step #5** – Connect with prospective customers. Taking off from that last line in the previous point, speak to your consumers and see what they have to say. Put up a questionnaire and conduct a proper survey to identify what customers have in mind; reach out to them personally and talk to them about what they want and what they receive. Try to listen to what their perceptions of the existing market are and what their opinions about the products currently available are. Ask them questions like –

- What makes you pick a particular company or brand to buy from?

- Do you return to that company to make purchases or do you buy the next time from someone else?

- Would you buy from our company if we were to offer you the same product even if we are only a start up?

These are just a few of the questions you should ask them. Make a full questionnaire and then once you receive the answers, quantify them into facts and figures. Draw out charts and diagrams that record their response and then statistically collate the data to make it easier to understand as well convince your stakeholders about the whole idea.

**Step #6** – Create a customer profile or a persona. Once you have collected all the data and collated it, you will find that the numbers automatically fall into different and very specific segments. Now, based on these segments, start building customer profiles.

Make sure you create profiles that are tangible and quantifiable. Given them a full, proper persona with names and characteristics like age, gender, income, etc. Make them real life people that you can target by describing them; create a written profile for them, full with their history, educational background, characteristics, etc.

Now for each segment of your target market, create a separate profile. You can even go, as far as to include images of this hypothetical person so that it makes it easier to envision them as a real person whose needs you must cater to.

This profile is your final consumer profile, as they currently exist. Remember, the market is in a constant state of flux and consumers keep changing – leave enough wiggle room in your profiles to be able to change according to the changing market trends and consumer demands.

When you have completed all these six steps, you will have built yourself the ideal customer profile and you will know exactly who your target market is. Add this to the overall market analysis report you have completed and you will be able to draft out a marketing strategy that helps you build your business better and allows you to create a loyal customer base and build brand loyalty.

# Market Analysis Report

Now, once you have completed this kind of a full Market Analysis, you must prepare a Market Analysis Report that will keep things clear and easy for you to understand. In the next chapter, we are going to take a look at where you can look for financers to back you and your venture. To convince them, you will need to prepare a full, detailed report of your entire business plan, with facts, figures, charts and diagrams that showcase all the research you have conducted. In the next chapter itself, I have given you an outline of a business plan and explained how to draft a basic plan – in it; you must definitely include the Market Analysis Report. This is one of the key aspects in your business plan that will go a long way in convincing potential investors that your venture is worth putting money in.

So here is a list of things you must include in your Market Analysis Report –

1. Description of the industry and your standing in relation to it. Outline what your industry is like currently, what the current market trends are and where it they seem to be headed. Add figures about industry metrics such as the size of the industry, projected growth rates, life cycles of the different companies, etc. Show your investors that you know the market you are stepping in to and then explain how you are prepared to handle it – identify

where you stand in this already established market and how you can capture your market share.

2. Description of your target market. This is where the consumer profile you built comes into play; by showing your investors a very realistic description of an audience that has been narrowed down, you will be able to convince them that you can build a good, loyal customer base that will not only return to you but also spread the word about your business and bring in more consumers. Make sure you include the following details in the description of your target market –

- User persona and characteristics such as their age, gender, location, income, etc. Include demographic, psychographic and other details so that your investors know who they are, what their buying habits and why they buy in the first place.

- Market size, including what share of the market you plan on capturing and the projected methods and time frame to do so; also include details about your competitors' market shares and how much your consumers are willing to spend annually on the product you sell – thus, what is the potential for growth for you?

3. Description of your competitive analysis. Obviously, you need to convince your investors that you will be able to capture the market share that you have projected within

your report. You must add facts and figures that will compare your standing with that of your competitors' and explain what you have to offer to your customers that your rivals do not have. Include the following details –

- Competitors' strengths and weaknesses; identify where they are lacking as well as where they stand strong. How will you deal with both of these qualities and how will you capitalize on opportunities they might oversee?

- Competitors' standing in the market and their market share; how much of the market have they captured? Who are their customers and do you have a plan to attract them to you instead?

- Barriers to entry; how many competitors are there that pose a barrier to your entry into the market? What is the cost of entry? Is it feasible? It is under this head that you must examine your own weaknesses in relation to your rivals – be honest in the report. Lying to look good is not only immoral; it will give you a bad image in front of your investors at a later stage when they find out the truth.

- Window of opportunity; when and where can you make your entry into the market? Is there a particular time frame within which you must do so? If yes, then what are the steps you must take to prepare yourself for the entry and how early must you start planning for it?

4. Description of projected facts and figures. As a start up company, you obviously have very few actual numbers to show your investors; you can only quote industry and research statistics. In relation to this, you must give them a projected earnings and numbers report that will quantify your idea further for them. If you want them to invest in you, you must get as specific as possible. Include the following –

- Market share and growth rate; after all the market analysis and research you have done, you should be able to identify what your potential market share can be and how much you will be able to grow in the next few years. Set a time frame for this projected growth and round even to a number you want to aim for. Keep the number practical and based on all your real life calculations instead of shooting in the dark; don't overreach, but do not underestimate your own potential either. Also give an explanation as to how you came up with these numbers – why do you think you will be able to reach this particular benchmark so easily?

- Pricing and profit margin; under this head, explain your pricing and cost structure and why you want to go with this particular pricing strategy. Discuss profitability, discounts you want to offer, competitive pricing strategies, etc. Identify the gross margin – this is the difference between your sales price and the cost of production you will incur. Also identify your break-even point; at what cost will you be able to make a proper profit instead of simply doing sales? Again, be honest and open about your numbers.

5. Description of any regulations you must adhere to. The market is an unpredictable place; you want to convince your investors that you are in the legal high ground and you are completely transparent in your operations. If there are any new market regulations that might pose an issue for smooth business operations, you must mention them in your report, along with solutions on how to deal with them. If there are specific rules set by the government that you must follow or standards you must adhere to, these have to be noted down here along with the procedures to be followed so that your investors know you are committed to being a good and proper entrepreneur on the right side of the law and in compliance with set standards within the industry.

All these headings must be included in your Market Analysis Report. Even if you are not meeting with potential investors and can manage your own finances, it is a good idea to complete this report – for two reasons. The first is that it will clarify things for you and show you how to move forwards. The second is that you will definitely need it to get your business legally registered with the concerned authorities for your license and to set up your business; you will need to convince them that you are serious about your venture and what better way to do it than this? You could also show your business plan, which, as I said, has been described in the next section.

# Chapter 5

## Where Will the Money for the Company Come from – Convincing Investors with a Good Business Plan

The money for your company will depend on the size and the type of the business that you own. If you have a business which is based out of your house, you will not require too much of money. The larger companies would require a lot of money for manufacturing and production. This chapter provides you with a few places you can go to in order to obtain the funding for your start – up.

Before we jump into whom you can approach for investment options, we need to first take a look at how you can convince them to spend money on you. Obviously, no investor will want to waste their hard earned cash; you must show them why you are good enough to invest and prove to them that your business venture is worth putting money into.

The problem with drafting a business plan is that most people assume that it is only for start-ups; this is not true. There are a number of different types of business plans, each catering to a particular aspect of business operation. You can have a sales plan, an operational and budget plan, a feasibility plan, a marketing plan and so on and so forth. Generally, though, a start up plan is easiest to write up, given that you have not actually begun working yet – your facts and figures will be projected numbers instead of actual figures and you will need to present evidence as to where, how and why you think these numbers will work for you.

You will need to include the Market Analysis Report from the previous section along with other details such as expenses incurred before launch, logo, website details, office and capital equipment (cost and other details) and most importantly – the available capital investment you already have in hand or the places you plan to arrange for it from. You will also need to include things like exit strategy for an investor who is not satisfied and how you will make use of the funds the investors do provide you with.

To make it easier, let me categorize a good business plan for you –

- *Executive Summary* – This is what you begin with; it is the first part of your plan and covers an overview of your entire venture and your strategy. Don't extend it beyond a page or two.

- *Company Overview* – These are the physical details of the company, from its legal structure to its location; include details like who the owners are, names and contacts of partners, etc.

- *Products and Services Offered* – What are you selling and why are you selling it? What is the production process and what are the costs and steps involved?

- *Market Analysis Report* – While a number of business plans tend to split this up into different heads such as Target Market, Milestones and Metrics, Market Trends and Competitors, etc., you can simply include the Market Analysis Report we worked on in the previous chapter. It provides all these details and more and is fully furnished with all numbers and projected statistics.

- *Marketing and Sales Plan* – The Market Analysis Report was based on the research you did; now you must include the marketing strategy you will adopt based on all the data collated. How will you reach your target audience and convince them to buy from you?

- *Management and Team* – This is where you can give details about employees, both current as well as those you plan to hire. As a start up, you'll probably have only a few employees at the get go, so what are you looking for in your future team? Whom do you need to hire and why?

- *Financial Forecast* – You've probably already mentioned a few of these details in your Market Analysis Report, but it never hurts to further quantify your terms in your business plan. Identify your cost and pricing structure and show graphs and data to project your break even point and the planned growth beyond that. Explain to each investor how every penny of theirs is going to be spent – be transparent so that they know where their money is going and will hence be willing to invest without hesitation.

- *Exit Strategy for Investor* – Remember some investors may decide to pull out later; you must provide them with a proper exit strategy, including all the legal details and enclosures.

- *Appendix* – Add any other product images or details or any extra information within this section and conclude your report.

Obviously, this is not a full stop guide for a business plan – you can include whatever other details and subheads you believe are important to convince your investors. Remember, business itself is a fluid field; what works for one venture may or may not work for another. So customize your business plan to suit your needs; this is simply a guideline you can follow to begin with. But do keep in mind the following tips to be convincing and professional –

- Keep it short and succinct. Nobody is interested in reading a 100 page plan; bulletin as much as possible so that it is easily accessible to everyone reading it and allows for changes to be made easily.

- Know your audience; keep the language easy to understand. For instance, if your product has a science based complex production process, you'll have to write your plan so that even layman investors (most certainly not scientists) will understand what you're talking about and be willing to invest. Cater to your investors' needs and they will return the favor. You can always add more specific detail in the appendix so that you're not accused of hiding anything in your attempt to keep it simple.

- Don't get intimidated by your prospective investors. People value confidence and wit; be open, honest and transparent in your dealings with your investors, but do not get intimidated and clam up in front of them. Remember, they may be business experts or they may not, but in the end, they are also learning and willing to go with the learning curve. Let your knowledge and passing for your business venture seep out; the more they see how hard you're willing to work for your company, the more willing they will be to invest in your venture.

Above all, be willing to listen to investors' ideas. Remember, a person who has a say in how things are run will definitely be more willing to spend money than someone who is cut out from the day to day of things. Be open and honest with them and be willing to listen to any ideas or changes they might suggest. That's not to say that you shouldn't reject them or let them take the reigns – continue to remain in control, but give them the option of exerting a little bit of power to. It will go a long way in convincing them to invest in your venture.

Once your business plan has been drafted out and you have made the necessary reports and facts and figures, you must be ready to approach your investors. Let us take a look at whom you can go to for funds to start your company.

## Your partners

Your partners can be a blessing to you and a curse to you. There is the advantage that when a lot of you are working together the load of the work becomes lighter. When you find someone whom you can trust with a set of skills that would benefit your company and are complementary to your skills, you will be glad to share the burden of finances. But, if you are looking at bringing in a person who is only going to be your partner and helps funding your business, you will have to remember that you are giving them the right to tell you about how your business must operate.

No matter what the circumstance may be, you will have to ensure that you have a partnership agreement that your lawyer draws up. You will have to talk to both your lawyer and your accountant, but it is always advisable to spread your business out if you choose to have one or more partners. This is best if you are willing to avoid any issues in the future.

Another aspect that you have to remember you will find it easy if you join hands with people and spread the initial costs. But, what happens when you have to start sharing the profits that you make? When you are struggling to fund your project at the initial stages, you will be glad to have someone to lend a hand. But, when you make a profit you would definitely not want to spread it amongst the partners.

## Grants

You have to remember that there are no grants that are available for you to help you when you start a business. There are quite a few grant books that are available online which will promise you a few million dollars which will help you start your firm up. But, these are not worth purchasing. This is for two reasons:

1. You will be able to obtain all the information you need from any sources from the government

2.  There is not too much money that is available for free

But, let me tell you something – there are some grants that the government is willing to give you. But, the grant will be given to you based on what type of a business yours is. You have to also ensure that your business does certain unique and special things.

## Loans

A lot of small businesses find it very difficult to obtain loans from the sources that are generally considered traditional. You should never consider going to a bank for a loan unless you have a good personal credit rating. You must also have a brilliant business plan. Even though, you will find it very difficult to obtain a loan from a bank unless you have a great rapport with the bank. You are very lucky if you are woman who has just started her own company. There are a lot of programs that aim at empowering women. You will have to focus on the different programs that are delivered in your province. You should work towards identifying those programs.

## The bank of Mum and Dad

There are a lot of entrepreneurs who have approached friends and acquaintances to obtain loans. But, there are a majority of the others who have approached their parents to help them out! You could do this by telling them that you would return their money, or provide them with partial partnership or write down a contract giving them a few of the shares in your company. This is always based on faith since your parents love you unconditionally. You would never have to give them the perfect business plan to convince them about your plan too!

## Creative Financing

There are quite a few companies over the world that has identified creative ways to finance their start – ups when the banks and other investors refused to give them any funds. Their ideas are quite amazing! You will need to think about the product that you can sell and see how much capital you can raise based on that product.

There are some people who have used creative ideas to sell their Harley Davidson motorcycles, their boats, their stamp collection, their vinyl records and houses too! When you find someone selling something that they really love or treasure, you know for a fact that they are sure about the idea that they are using for their start – up. The bank managers are always impressed when they find the potential clients putting their assets up as a guarantee for the loan.

There was an entrepreneur who was very creative! There was a lady a few years ago who had collected different departmental store credit cards. She used these cards to buy products in the market and then convinced the male clerk to take all the goods back. This is not something that I recommend that you do, since these cards charge an interest.

# Chapter 6

# Market and Sales Strategies

Every small businessman always waits to seize the idea that is the most popular during the phase when they are setting up their company. The owners of small businesses tend to be the worst at this since they are always performing a hundred other things at once! The most important thing that any small business owner will want is the marketing plan!

The important thing to remember is that a business owner can use a million tactics to ensure that his company performs consistently if he or she has obtained the right marketing strategy. This is why the part where you identify the strategy holds utmost importance. There are two components to identifying the marketing strategy for your business. The first is to bring your focus down to the one client who would match the characteristics of an ideal client. The other one is to work on differentiating your business from the rest. This may not be an idea that will make your dreams come true, but the truth is that when you think correctly about it, you will be able to understand why they hold the highest importance.

Now you may notice that a lot of the following ideas are repeated from the previous sections – this is because the idea of marketing research begins even before you set your company up and continues all the way into growth and expansion. As I have said before, market research and analysis must take place consistently, simultaneously and constantly so that you remain on top of your game and continue to be successful in your endeavors.

## Part One: Defining your ideal client

There are a lot of businesses that have worked towards becoming everything that the client wanted them to be. The business owners then found it difficult to focus on their company and they find it difficult to serve the smallest segments of the market. The owners do not want to be everything that the consumers want, but they tend to lose focus because they want to help every person who comes knocking on their door. This characteristic is not one that a businessman should have.

It is good to take on new customers, but if the customer turns out to be bad you will find that your company has stopped growing. You will find yourself in bad situations when you are trying to please a customer who was never an ideal customer to your business. You will find your business crashing because of the customer's reviews about your company.

Most businesses, whether large or small, have been built with the sole idea to cater to a segment of the market. This does not imply that the market will never grow or change or evolve. But, you will have to identify the ideal customers even when your company is growing.

The trick that you will have to learn is to identify what your ideal client will look like. Write down all the characteristics of your ideal client and then build your strategy around those characteristics. You will find yourself attracting more customers with the same characteristics. There are certain businesses that only look at the set of people who will be able to afford the products and services that they offer.

However, there are other business owners who will view his ideal client as someone who has a lot of other people he will introduce to the business. It is always good to find people who will work well with the company and the owner. There will be miserable outcomes otherwise.

The perfect fit would be one where the customer who has approached you finds solace in the help that you provide him with. There is also the meaning that the customer values the way you approach the problem and the way you treat the client. If you choose someone just because he can pay you for the products and services that you offer you will eventually find them sucking the life out of your business.

More often than not, a client who is not ideal is a person whom the company would love to work with. But, there is a catch here – the company will not be able to help the client. For instance, let us assume that you have a friend who has always wanted to give back to the society. He or she has started to work for an organization. But, when he or she begins to work they find it difficult to mold themselves according to certain rules stated by the organization since they do not agree with them. This would make them a bad fit for the organization.

There are five steps that have been given below which will help you identify your ideal clients from your current client base.

1. You have to first find the clients who have been most profitable to you

2. In the group that you have identified above, you will have to find the people who have referred you to their friends.

3. From the second group that you have created identify the group from the common regions

4. Take some time to understand them better and see what you can do in order to help them and understand what makes them ideal.

5. Now draw a complete sketch of the ideal customer, which you can use while writing your marketing guide.

We have already seen how you can classify these clients based on different factors such as demography, psychography and the like. Now that you have begun actual sales, compare your actual facts and figures to the projected numbers you came up with in your earlier Market Analysis Report. See where the difference lies and if you are lagging behind, identify the factors that are causing this dissonance. Also identify steps that you can take to make up for the difference.

## Part Two: Differentiate the Business

Every small business must identify a way by which they will be able to stand out. They have to identify ways to differentiate their company from the rest of the companies that perform the same functions as them. This is not a new concept but is definitely the hardest for any company to do.

Every person has the notion that what they are doing is unique. This is unfortunate since most companies that perform the same functions do proclaim the same thing as well. But there is a way by which you will be able to grasp the idea. Since you have identified your competitors, you would also have access to their websites. Copy the information that has been given in the 'About Us' page for five companies. You will find that the information that is in the paragraphs is similar!

The best way to identify what makes you unique is by conducting an interview of your customers. Here are a few questions you can ask them.

1. Why did you choose our company?

2. What is it about us that you prefer over the other companies?

3. What do you think is the one thing that we can do better?

4. Would you be willing to refer our company to any other person?

5. If you were to refer us to someone, how would you describe us?

When you ask your customers these questions, you will be able to identify the differences between your company and your competitors. You will have to try to identify the common views of the customers and develop a message that you would use to market. This message should support the views of your existing customers. This is not very easy since you will have to ensure that you are not like everyone else. You have to be different! You may have noticed that people in an industry always tend to talk in the same way about their products and services. It is because of this that small business owners believe that they have to do the same! But, you have to ensure that you step out of the box! This is a hard thing for you to do, but it will prove to be the best for your company!

## Different Marketing Strategies

There are a lot of different strategies that you could use to market your products and services. This section of the chapter covers a few of these strategies.

## Word of Mouth

This is the simplest strategy, but also the hardest and the trickiest. This is because of the fact that your customers spread the word about your company. If you have one disgruntled customer, you will probably have a bad name in the market. This is because the word will spread like fire! If you satisfy a consumer, you will find yourself gaining more consumers since the satisfied consumer would have referred your company to them.

## Advertisements

Different companies to help in creating a market plan for their company have used advertisements. You could find different ways by which you can promote your products and services. You could use newspapers to billboards and leaflets and pamphlets.

The best way to market your products and services is through videos. The most common platform was YouTube. When you have identified the best way to market your product, you will need to be able to answer the following questions:

1. How much would you have to spend for the method you have chosen?

2. Is there a particular way that you would want to market the product? What type of an advertisement are you looking at? Are you looking at a particular color?

3. Are you looking at different types of ideas at once?

4. Do you want the advertisement to run for a month or for a week?

## Direct marketing

This is an easy way to promote the products and services you offer. This would happen only when you directly communicate with your potential customers. You can talk to them via email or have a conversation over the telephone. You could also meet them at their place or meet them at a convention or a trade. You could also leave them an email or a letter about the products and services that you sell. You will however have to give them all the details about the product and service that you are providing for your customers.

## Social Media Marketing

Social media marketing is the best way to promote the products and services that you offer. This is a method that is free of cost! You will however have to be very creative about how you can market your products and services on social media. You will find that you are able to approach a huge network.

You will find that it is easier to interact with your consumers on a regular basis if you are active on social media. You will find yourself being able to provide them with services on the go. You will be able to use quite a few platforms to market the products and services that you are providing for your customer. You could use social networks like Facebook and Twitter as well. These platforms are essentially for start – up companies.

## Website

When it comes to a website, you do not have to be too worried. You would have wondered about the different tabs that you would have to create on your website to explain the details about your company. But, you do not have to complicate your website at all! You could have just a few pages on your website, but these have to explain what your company does in detail. You have to also ensure that you give the customers a chance to contact you when they want to. You can always work towards making your website mobile friendly which will ensure that a larger number of people will look at your website.

Once you have identified your strategy you will have to begin working on your business plan. Your business plan will need to cover every aspect about your company right from hat your company does to the market strategies that you are going to use for to promote your products and services.

# Chapter 7

# The 10 Step Guide to Starting Your Very Own Business!

This chapter gives you the gist of what you will need to do in order to start a successful business! You will need to keep all of these points in mind when you are working on your strategies. This could be your very own checklist where you could strike a certain step off once you are certain that you have completed it! The previous chapters have helped you understand the different ways by which you will be able to complete the steps given below.

## Step 1 – Testing your business idea

This is a very important step. When you have decided about what your business has to be, you will have to identify different ways to test the idea. You could use various tools that are available online to test your idea. You will also have to assess your skills since your skills are vital for your business to flourish. When you have decided what your company is about, you will have to think about how the products and services will be looked at by your potential customers. You have to be able to answer questions about how the products and services that you are providing the customers will benefit them.

## Step 2 – Conducting Market Research

Most entrepreneurs formulate their ideas based on a certain product or service that they have seen or used. When you have tested your idea, you will have to see if the products and services that you are providing are any different from other businesses in the same market – your competitors. Through market research you will be able to identify the population that you would want to target. For instance, if you are looking at setting up a company that sells woolen products, you will have to approach the areas around the world where it is cold most of the time. When you conduct thorough research, you will know whether the location or the idea you have chosen will be profitable to you.

## Step 3 – Understanding your business requirements

You would have identified the product and service that you would want to provide to your potential customers based on your market research. You will also be able to zero in on a location that would be best suited for your venture. When you have settled on the location, you would have to identify a place where you would be able to produce or manufacture your products. You will therefore, need to list down all the raw material and equipment you will require in while setting up a successful business. Every company needs labor – both manual and technological – in order for it to function. You will have to identify the cost and the number of people you would need to employ. When you set up a business, you will have certain additional expenses or overhead expenses that are required to have a successful company. You may have to buy insurance in order to protect yourself from any risk!

## Step 4 – Understanding the requirements for investment

You would have been able to identify the costs that you will incur when you have set your business up. But, there are certain costs that you will incur when you are beginning your business – the starting costs – and also while the business is running-running costs. Once you have identified your costs, you will have to identify different ways by which you will be able to finance these costs. You could approach different Government agencies to support you with the funding or approach Banks and other Unions to provide you with financial support.

## Step 5 – Identifying your market strategy

This is an important step! You may have the best idea about what services and products your company provides, but if you do not market these products and services the right way, you will not be able to create a successful business. You will have to work towards identifying the perfect strategy by looking at the different strategies that have been used by similar companies in the market. You will have to ensure that you are choosing a strategy that is cost effective. When you are done identifying your plan, you will need to write it down in order to present it to an investor or an employee in your company.

## Step 6 – Working on your sales plan

This is a crucial step for your business. When you have defined your product and service, you will also have to look at how you will promote it. This is done in the previous step. But, when you are promoting your product, you will have to ensure that you have your target market in mind. Before you promote your product and service at a location, you will have to identify the perfect way by which you will be able to distribute your products and services as requested by your customers. As for the profitability of your company, you will need to fix on a selling price and will also have to settle for a break – even point which will help you determine your profit!

## Step 7 – Identify the type of company

In the former chapters of the book, you learnt about the different types of businesses that exist in the market. You will need to identify the perfect business for you since – sole trader or proprietor, partnership or a limited company. This will help in giving you an idea about the legal structure for your business.

## Step 8 – Identify your risks!

When you are looking at starting a business, you will realize that it is a big step that you have taken; in fact, it is not a big step but a leap! It is an exciting thing to do and gives you an adrenaline rush since you have decided to do something on your own. But, there is a possibility of a risk. You will have to identify what risks you may face in the future or at the present. Some people may consider personal funding a huge risk while others may consider securing employment a risk. It is always good to identify and estimate the level of risk when you are looking at starting a business.

## Step 9 – Try to adhere to the rules

It is always good to abide by the rules that have been stated by a government or a governing body. If they require that you be registered under a Company's Act, you better be! If you fail to adhere to the rules that have been provided to you, you are leading your company into facing unnecessary risks. You have to also ensure that your employees are treated right.

## Step 10 – Create your very own business plan!

This is a fundamental step that you must check off your list since this will lead to the success of your business. When you create your business plan, you know what you had aimed for. You will be able to know how you want to manage the company and will be able to project your required sales and profit. When you create a plan, you have the power in your hand to ensure that things get done the way they were supposed to. You will find that you are able to make the right decisions and will be able to manage your business effectively.

# Recommended Product

As a start – up you would have to identify a platform that will work towards promoting your product. I recommend that you use the Amazon Web Services, which will help you start your business and let it scale up to its heights. It has the best interface and does not cost too much!

# Conclusion

Thank you for purchasing the book.

As a person who is breaking away from tradition and starting a new company, you would need a great amount of help. You would have quite a few questions in your head about whether or not you will succeed. This book washes all your scares away. It guides you through every step that you will need to go through in order to set up a successful business.

You may not have an idea about what business that you would want to start. There is a chapter in the book that has provided you with the best ideas that you can use to begin your start up. You will have to always test the idea that you have in your mind before you launch it into the market. The third chapter in the book covers the different methods you could use to test your idea.

The rest of the book covers the different strategies that you could use in order to generate good revenue. When you decide on your business, you will have to conduct research to know what your competitors are like. The fourth chapter in the book gives you a proper explanation on how you can do this. The one thing that may be haunting you is where your money will come from! You have been given different sources from where you will be able to gain a lot of money. You have also been given a few strategies that you could use in order promote your product. The last chapter leaves you with a perfect guide that you could use as a checklist!

Remember that it is all right to make a mistake the first time! You will be able to achieve success over time. Take baby steps and keep pushing yourself forward!

Thank you for purchasing the book. I hope it helped you!

If you received value from this book, then I would like to ask you for a favor. Would you be kind enough to leave a review for this book on Amazon?

Thank you so much!

Made in the USA
Monee, IL
26 November 2020

49640627R00059